思考は思考をもたらす

思考は人生のすべてを支配します

際限なく閉じ込められた

【ミクコンセプト】

Miku Suzuki

Love and illusions

Zen aphorisms

Bibliografische Information
der Deutschen
Nationalbibliothek: Die
Deutsche Nationalbibliothek
verzeichnet diese Publikation
in der Deutschen
Nationalbibliografie;
detaillierte bibliografische
Daten sind im Internet
über dnb.dnb.de abrufbar.

【ミクコンセプト】

Herstellung und Verlag:

BoD – Books on Demand,
Norderstedt

ISBN: 9783754327258

Hope

Love seen quickly and think
the day well, sentences invert
my world, just live through
the day.

Love

Well have squeezed the
construct, catch the good
thoughts of life.

Playful

Reinvent old thoughts, feel
briefly secure and talk to
yourself, hope.

Tears

The tear sticks to the face, the
thoughts stick to life with the
tear and hit you.

Illusion

The illusion of knowledge
constricts my good love of life
and I breathe.

By mistake

Fine tones arise from the
tones and hope gets an
additional narrowing and the
believed love warms.

Base

A very good basis for living is
to believe better without
being caught, by yourself or
by others.

Beliefs

Orientation to the beliefs
helps to reach the apparent
goal and die.

Awareness

The stench from the mouth
opens a new world and
captures everyone.

Love

Just the word love has a great
meaning and likes to take us
to an innocent world and
unfortunately turns us around.

Illusion

Useful things are good for us
and must not be lost until the
end.

Finally

Finally takes us to an infinity,
let's look at love, gladly we
just take over everything.

Hope

The good hope of the stupid
shocks us and makes us think,
because performance counts
and that brings us I to the
goal.

The death

Innocent death invades life
and I wonder.

Blooming

Briefly my mind blossoms,
looks at faces and takes the
beautiful spirit, all seems well.

Comfort

I comfort you and find no
end, the wise men impatiently
chide.

Excitement

Excited we run blindly to our
doom, breathe in briefly and
simply age.

Deception

Currently you have to be clear
and endure a lot of pain so
that you can go to heaven and
finally be happy there.

Start

The day starts well, no one
heard a contradiction, it hasn't
been this quiet for days, and
already made another mistake.

Sense

Forget everything and be
cheerful for no reason and
blame the others.

Joy in life

Using days well and achieving
a lot and slipping again with
the thoughts that arise, useful
but useless.

Contradictions

In recognition lies a great
mystery and yet it is forgotten
the next day.

Henchman

Break the fist of enemies and
become powerless, give up
life and happiness suddenly
comes flying and creates a
new image.

Love

The breaking love remains in
the thoughts, the illusion is
strengthened.

Food

Hastily gulping down food
and being an epicurean, that's
all happiness is, being an
epicurean

Liberation

Meditating out of weariness
and hoping for final liberation
from destructive thoughts,
having good opinions.

Contradiction

Again finding the
contradiction of the good
righteous to vomit.

Where to

Not being at home in the
heart, standing in the
elsewhere and hoping for
enlightenment today turns all
mysticism into excrement.

Trust

Showing the right laugh at the
right time and showing up on
time for your own funeral.

Dreams

Letting thoughts dance in
your head, breathing in the
scent of lust, sweating and
being a dreamer.

Winner

Since I won, I can now call myself a winner and a great person.

About

The clouds in the sky fly a lot today, memorized the day, the past I am now, be a beau and laugh madly.

See

For good reasons, the supervisor could not say anything, any responsibility lay with the others, and love was now also a word often said.

Quick

The blackbird on the
windowsill chirps me a
morning song and I have to
quickly put on my pants and
do my routine even faster.

From

How often may I still play
with thoughts to understand
me, play with life and finally
want to be redeemed, good
thoughts are also just
thoughts.

Responsibility

I have given up responsibility,
it's really none of my business
anymore, just like you.

Maggot

The maggot spreads in my
mind, it gets fatter, eventually
finds a home and stays with
me for the rest of my life.

Heart muscle

With an empty heart I meet
my heart muscle, with an
empty heart I meet your
brain, with an empty heart I
meet being.

Imprisoned

Seeing life in the prison of
love, being very safe and
seemingly happy to be locked
up.

Love

Forgetting the self in the
thirst for love, wanting to be
good and already thinking and
sinking.

Please

And we ask and hope, poetry
stories, being in the prison of
dreams, being in the prison of
love.

Yesterday

A good morning brings back
faith, a good evening makes
you die short, the days stay in
your head, simplicity
disappears.

Birth

Always a new birth and always
getting older, always dying
anew.

Fear

Fear has aged you, but the
good days will never be over.

Freedom

To be afraid or to be free,
spring will come every year, to
you and to me.

Faces

The faces stare at me, they
wanted to give me hope, I
don't have time and I long for
solitude back.

Hold on

To wise sentences we hold on
forever, they also give a hope,
let us stray.

Emptied

Finally found the void and
suddenly get nightmares
again, curse the wise and
recognize trust as an illusion.

Miracles

The miracles of the heart heal you, take proper care of the wounds and become vain with them.

Suffering

Suffering may not always have great meaning, but for transformation, suffering always has meaning and gives you a chance.

Familiarity

Understand the confidence in my thoughts and make it a consolidated idea.

Frozen

Joy overcomes me and I
notice the excitement inside
me that continues and yet falls
silent.

Sounds

The ringing and the seemingly
absolute silence hit you briefly
and disappear with the first
thought of success.

Courageously

Courageously embrace the
consciousness of success and
become strong and conquer
and murder and finally be a
whole person.

Excited

Aroused is not excited and comes from somewhere, but has something to do with unreasonableness and attacks you spontaneously, makes you feel life.

Light

Standing upright and thinking of the light of a candle, thinking of the unbelievable possible cheerfulness and being happy.

Fruits

I found you, you make me ripen and also rot, I love you and age in thought.

Vomit

The vomit of the friendly
drunk sticks to my jacket,
drives away my love for
understanding and existence.

Puswimmerl

Your face and your speeches
full of Eiterwimmerl makes
me shudder and suddenly I
am simply in Dasein.

Slain

You imprison me with your
superiority and I just keep on
dreaming.

Deception

When the door of heaven
opened and the great sage
entered, he stumbled
foolishly.

Kindnesses

To be kind again and lovingly
embrace the nonsense and be
free for a moment.

Dying

The great difference in dying
shows everyone that there is
no difference at all, we
reproduce and die.

Language

The well-chosen sentence and clever response invite laughter and levity.

Balanced

Sitting on the floor well consolidated and laughing and regaining what is right, who is really right.

Determine

Be very happy and be very kind, the beginning is made, you have the task to find yourself again and be happy.

Weight

The weight of thoughts pulls
me into my grave, deeper and
deeper, only the grave waits
for you.

Heart

Permeated by love, by
dreaming and thinking out
loud and even louder, and
finally saying something
smart.

Swap

Exchanging life in the head,
good and bad thoughts,
feelings and hard knowledge,
beliefs and joys and oneself.

Jump off

Jump off once and win it all,
have won forever and then
run away.

Small

Staring at the sun, inventing a
new day, staying optimistic
and friendly, that already
hurts, praising the sun, being
wistful and very friendly.

Web

Being caught in thinking,
waiting for explanations,
searching for the right
meaning.

Direct

Spitting out the last thought
without consideration and
being ruthless is a timeless
good character trait.

Promise

Not having promised
anything and not knowing the
center of the earth despite
great humility, not being able
to accomplish anything,
coming here and giving up.

Admonisher

Slowly the admonitions of the
sage fade away, the sage has
become old and thin and
stupid.

Groundless

There is no real reason to
accumulate great knowledge
or to be wise.

Lost

To be completely lost, by no
means to be alone, but to
simply want to be there and
be at peace.

Happiness

A happiness I found briefly,
having control over my
worlds, a good happiness, a
good illusion.

Order

Anyone who has received an
order from wise men, carries
it out properly and is proud of
it, must be a liar.

Lies

Lied to and destroyed
everything, you must be the
exemplary strong one.

Miracles

There are no new miracles
after all, the known ones must
be enough and you will find
yourself.

Imagination

Imagination has a beautiful function, to imagine hope, to brighten the day.

Realization

I could not see the meaning of happiness and foolishly rejoiced.

Slowly

Slowly come back to one's senses and be a good person, calm the conscience and be a good member of the righteous.

Thinking

Thought too much and didn't
see the con, nodded to
everyone and hoped for
confirmation, thought on, all
done well.

End

An end, an end to the year
and an end to life, all found
without effort.

Noise

The noise in the head has
become music, be kind to all,
be good.

Bill

Having to pay everything, no
bill goes unpaid, gifts are
dangerous and the wish
fulfilled will later seem like a
punishment.

Shortcut

As the shortcuts became a
habit, you go through a
tedious life on the short paths.

Calculated

To have calculated well, to be
a clever head, to have seen
well, and yet to come to ruin.

Words

There will always be words,
words that describe all of life.

Door

The calm has opened briefly,
the restlessness comes back
and everything else is
unimportant, find a quiet
place.

Begin

Start now, do the work and
have earned the pleasure of it,
every day new, without
thinking much.

Vanity

Grabbing you by your vanity
and watching you die, fall
down and get back up.

Laughter

And shine the thought that
many hope to catch.

Love

Love must not be forgotten,
the love of nothingness, the
love of emptiness and the
love of being.

これが最後のページです

言うことは何も残っていません

私が言えることはすべて
延々と言われてきました

思考は思考をもたらす
最後の考えが魂と共に逃げるまで

その後、すべてが無料で純粋です